THE SECOND BOOK OF SOPRANO SOLOS

compiled by Joan Frey Boytim

ISBN 978-0-7935-3799-0

G. SCHIRMER, Inc.

DISTRIBUTED BY

HAL•LEONARD®
CORPORATION

7777 W. BLUEMOUND RD. P.O. BOX 13819 MILWAUKEE, WI 53213

PREFACE

The eight volumes that comprise "The First Book of Solos" and "The First Book of Solos—Part II" were compiled to provide a great variety of song literature at the same basic level of difficulty for students at the beginning stages of voice study. The four volumes in "The Second Book of Solos" are designed to contribute to musical and vocal development at the next progressive level of study.

The majority of these songs require more vocal sophistication than those found in the earlier volumes. Singers using this set will be exposed to songs with wider ranges that require more vocal flexibility and vocal control, and that make greater use of the dramatic qualities of the voice. The student who can sing many of the songs in the "The First Book" and "The First Book—Part II" will be ready for the challenges found in "The Second Book of Solos."

The general format of songs remains the same as the previous collections, with a representative group of songs in English, Italian, German, and French from various periods of music history, as well as selected sacred solos. Added are several songs from Gilbert and Sullivan operettas and solos from the oratorio repertoire. Numerous pieces previously available only in single sheet form and many songs that for some time have been out of print are included.

I want to thank Richard Walters for encouraging the development of this practical song literature series. The twelve books, taken together, provide a comprehensive, inexpensive collection of 400 songs for the voice teacher and student.

Joan Frey Boytim

About the Compiler...

Since 1968, Joan Frey Boytim has owned and operated a full-time voice studio in Carlisle, Pennsylvania, where she has specialized in developing a serious and comprehensive curriculum and approach to teaching and coaching adolescent and community adult students. Her teaching experience has also included music and choral instruction at the junior high and senior high levels, and voice instruction at the college level. She is the author of the widely used bibliography, *Solo Vocal Repertoire for Young Singers* (a publication of NATS), and, as a nationally recognized expert on teaching beginning vocal study, is a frequent speaker and clinician on the topic.

CONTENTS

ART IS CALLING FOR ME

(The Prima Donna Song)

from *The Enchantress* (1911)

Harry B. Smith

Victor Herbert

MINA:

Mam-ma is a queen, and pa-pa is a king; So
I'm in the é-lite, and men sigh at my feet; Still

I I am a Prin-cess, I ___ know it; But
I do not fan-cy my po-si-tion; I

court et-i-quette is a dull drear-y thing, I just
have not much use for the men that I meet, I quite

8va

hate it all, _____ and I show it.
burn with lyr - ic am - bi - tion.

To
Those

sing on the stage, that's the one life for me,
ten - ors so sweet, if they made love to me,

My
I'd

fig - ure's just like Te - traz - zi - ni; _____
be a suc - cess, that I do know; _____

I
And

know I'd win fame if I sang in "Bo - hème;"
Mel - ba I'd oust If I once sang in "Faust,"

That
That

op - 'ra by Sig - nor Puc - ci - ni. I've rou -
op - 'ra so charm - ing by Gou - nod. Girls would

Poco meno

lades and the trills that would send the cold chills down the
be on the brink of hys - ter - ics, I think, e - ven

Pesante

backs of all hear - ers of my vo - cal frills. _____
strong men would have to go out for a drink. _____

colla voce

REFRAIN:

I long to be a pri - ma
I long to be a pri - ma

7

8

peach - y can - ta - *tri - ce,   like   oth - er **plump girls that I
"Vi - va" to the   di - va,   oh,   ver - y   love - ly that must

see; _____   I   hate so -
be; _____   That's what I'm

ci - e - ty;   I   hate pro - pri - e - ty;
dy - ing for,   That's what I'm sigh - ing for,

(D.C.)

Art   is call - ing for   me. _____
Art   is call - ing for   me. _____

* treechy
** optional lyric: "Songbirds" replacing "plump girls"

BESCHEIDENE LIEBE

(Modest Heart)

Hugo Wolf
English translation by John Bernhoff

1. Ich bin wie an - dre Mäd - chen nicht, die, wenn sie lie - ben,
1. I'm not as o - ther las - sies are, who, when in love, are

schwei - gen und ihr Ge - heim - nis hü - tend stumm, das kran - ke Köpfchen
si - lent, and hang their head, and hot tears shed, I'm some-what of a

nei - gen. Ja, mei - ne Lie - be ist nicht stumm, mein Plau - dern geb' ich
ty - rant. The neigh - bours see us e - very day, my heart is light and

12

hat mich schon lieb Müt - ter - lein mit dem Herz - al - ler - lieb - sten mein beim
oft has mo - ther's watch - ing eye just caught me kiss - ing him "Good bye," that's

Ko - sen an - ge - trof - fen, beim Ko - sen an - ge - trof - fen.
bet - ter far than hop - ing, or sit - ting there and mop - ing.

3. Ich bin wie an - dre Mäd - chen nicht, doch glück - lich, wie ich glau - be, denn
3. I'm not as o - ther las - sies are, yet hap - py, who dare doubt it? A

LES CLOCHES

(The Bells)

Paul Bourget
translation by Isabella G. Parker

Claude Debussy

warn - ing, A - far through the air, Bring - ing mem - 'ry
en - ne, Ce loin - tain ap - pel Me re - mé - mo -

sweet of lil - ies a - dorn - ing Ho - ly al - tar
rait la blan - cheur chré - tien - ne Des fleurs de l'au -

rit. e dim.

fair.
tel.

poco meno mosso
(un peu plus lent)

dolce ed espress.
(doux et expressif)

These bells tell of hap - py years now o'er -
Ces clo - ches par - laient d'heu - reu - ses an -

DIE NACHT
(Night)

Herrmann von Gilm
translation by Isabella G. Parker

Richard Strauss

DOWN IN THE FOREST

Harold Simpson

Landon Ronald

Più lento e con molto espressione.

Now in the morn- ing of life I__ stand And I long for the touch of your

hand; _____ I am__ here, I am here at your door, Oh

love, oh,__ love, we will wait no__

more! _____

FIOCCA LA NEVE

(Snow)

Giovanni Pascoli
English version by
Lorraine Noel Finley

Pietro Cimara

Molto moderato

Len - ta la ne - ve fioc - ca, fioc - ca,
Slow-ly the star - ry flakes of snow are

fioc - ca._____ Sen - ti, u - na za - na don-do-la pian pia - no._____
fall - ing._____ Lis-ten to a cra - dle rhyth-mi-cal-ly swing - ing._____

poco cresc.

Un bim - bo pian - ge, il pic-ciol di - to in boc - ca._____
Fe-vered, a child is tear-ful-ly wake-ful, call - ing;_____

di - no._____
found   you."_____

Nel bel giar - di - no il bim - bo s'ad - dor - men - ta,_____
Cov-ered with flow'rs, the child's young heart is drift - ing._____

fioc - ca la ne - ve len - ta, len - ta, len - ta,_____ fioc - ca la
Slow-ly the snow is fall - ing, slow - ly sift - ing,_____ Qui - et - ly

ne - ve,_____ fioc - ca la ne - ve._____
fall - ing,_____ qui - et - ly drift - ing._____

HARK! THE ECHOING AIR

Henry Purcell
Arranged by John Reed

29

HEAR MY PRAYER, O LORD

from the Biblical Songs

Psalms 61 and 63

Antonín Dvořák

I will dwell_ for - ev - er in Thy tents_ and hide me in the shad - ow of Thy wings.

Lord!_ Thou art in - deed my God,

yea, I will seek Thee ear - ly. My soul is faint, my

bod - y long - eth, long - eth aft - er Thee

in a bar - ren de - sert where there is no wa - ter.

Now I will bless Thee dai - ly and lift my hands in pray'r and ad - o - ra - tion; yea, my lips shall praise Thee all my life long.

VILLANELLE

(I Saw the Swift Swallow Flying)

F. van der Elst
English by Alice Mattullath

Eva Dell'Acqua

*) Breathe here eventually, when singing the high version.

But in vain my soul was cry - ing
Et j'au - rais vou - lu comme el - le

for the land the swal - low knows,
Suiv - re le mê - me che - min,

I saw the swift swal - low
J'ai vu pas - ser l'hi - ron

fly - ing seek - ing sum - mer that un dy - - - - ing
del - le, Elle al - lait à ti - re d'ai - - - - le

fly - ing seek - ing sum - mer that un - dy - - - - ing,
del - le, 'Elle al - lait à ti - re d'ai - - - - le,

LOVE'S PHILOSOPHY

Shelley

Roger Quilter

Printed in the U.S.A. by G. Schirmer, Inc.

MEIN GLÄUBIGES HERZE

(My Heart Ever Faithful)

Johann Sebastian Bach

45

46

UN MOTO DI GIOJA

(A Moment of Joy)

English Version by Joan Boytim

Wolfgang Amadeus Mozart

MY HEART IS LIKE A SINGING BIRD

Christina Rossetti

C. Hubert H. Parry

-cause the birth-day of my life is come,_____

_____ My love_____ is come_____ to

me.

SHEPHERD! THY DEMEANOUR VARY

Thomas Brown
arranged by H. Lane Wilson

Shep-herd! thy de - mean - our va - ry, Dance and sing,— be

light ____ and air - y, Dance ____

____ and sing, Dance, ____ be .

light ____ and air - y, Dance, ____ be

light ____ and air - y.

colla voce   *ff*   *Presto*

O DIVINE REDEEMER

Charles Gounod

Molto moderato

Ah!__ turn me not a - way,__ re - ceive me, tho' un-

wor - thy, Ah!__ turn me not a - way,__ re - ceive me, tho' un-

wor - thy! Hear Thou my cry, hear Thou my cry, be - hold, Lord, my dis-

pray Thee, grant me__ par - - don,__ and re-mem-ber not, remember not, O

Lord, my sins! Night gath-ers round my soul;____

fear - ful, I cry to Thee;____ Come to mine aid, O Lord!____

Haste Thee, Lord, haste to help me! Hear my cry,____

par - - don — and re - mem-ber not, re-mem-ber not, O Lord, my

sins! Save, in the day of ret - ri - bu - - tion, from

Death shield Thou me, O my God!____ O, di - vine Re - deem - er, have

mer - cy! Help me, my Sav - ior!

OH! HAD I JUBAL'S LYRE

Allegro. (♩ = 100.)   from Joshua   George Frideric Handel

Printed in the U.S.A. by G. Schirmer, Inc.

faint - ly show How much to heav'n and thee I owe, My

hum - ble strains but faint - ly show How much to heav'n and

largamente

thee I owe, how much to heav'n and thee I owe. Tempo I.

col canto

A PASTORAL

from Rosalinda

Francesco Maria Veracini
(1690-c1750)

long - er then de - lay. Ah! _____
lab - bro av - ve - le - nar. Ah! _____

colla voce　　　　　　　　　　*colla voce*

O - ver the hill - tops yon - der, Come,
Me - co ver - rai su quel - la, A -

rit. colla voce

dear - est, let us wan - der, Come, dear - est, let us
- me - na col - li - net - ta, A me - na col - i -

wan - - - - der: There on my pipe I'll play, _____ And
- net - - - - ta; Li - be - ra pas - tor - el - la, L'a -

SLEEP, GENTLE CHERUB, SLEEP DESCEND

from the oratorio Judith

Isaac Bickerstaff

Thomas Arne

And o'er his sa - cred temp - les bend, bend, O bend their sa - lu - ta - ry

shade. O gent - le Che - rub, O sleep descend, descend, thy healing wings pro -

tec - tive spread, and o'er his sa - cred temp - les bend, O bend thy shade, thy sa - lu -

ta - ry shade O bend thy sa - lu - ta - ry shade.

SONG OF THE BLACKBIRD

W.E. Henley

Roger Quilter

espressivo.
Black-bird plays but a box-wood flute,.......... But I
mp
vivo delicato.
dolce.
love him, I love him best of all
mf vivo
Ped.
mf Poco più allegro e con moto.
For his song is all of the
L.H.
f
mf
Ped.
joy of life, And we in the
Ped.

A SPRING MORNING

Henry Carey
arranged by H. Lane Wilson

Ah!_____ Joy and pleas - ure

with-out meas - ure Her - alds in____ the love - ly spring,

Her-alds in____ the love - ly spring. La la la la la__

la__ la_____ La la la la la__ la__ la_____

streams and cool - ing_ shades, Sen-ses charm - ing,

pains dis - arm - ing, Love each ten - der heart in-vades.

Danc-ing, sing - ing,

pi-ping, spring - ing, With our mirth the val-leys ring.

Ah!

Ah! Joy and

pleas - ure with-out meas - ure Her - alds in___ the

love - ly spring, Her-alds in___ the love - ly spring.

colla voce

a tempo
mf

THE SUN WHOSE RAYS

from The Mikado

words by W. S. Gilbert

music by Arthur Sullivan

Andante commodo

PIANO

mf

p sostenuto

The sun, whose rays Are all a - blaze With ev - er liv - ing glo - ry,

Does not de - ny His ma - jes - ty He scorns to tell a sto - ry!

He won't ex-claim "I blush for shame, So kind-ly be in - dul - gent."

91

THE SUN SHALL BE NO MORE THY LIGHT

Dr. Maurice Greene

TAKE, O TAKE THOSE LIPS AWAY

William Shakespeare

Amy Beach

Andantino con espressione

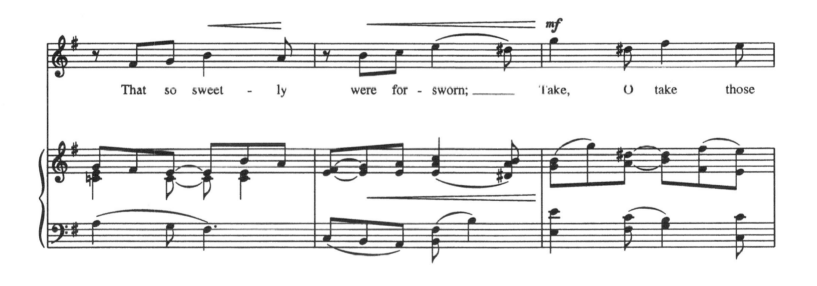

THESE ARE THEY WHICH CAME

from The Holy City

Alfred Robert Gaul

VERGEBLICHES STÄNDCHEN

(The Vain Suit)

Anton Wilhelm Florentin von Zuccalmaglio
English version by Henry Chapman

Johannes Brahms

DAS VERLASSENE MÄGDLEIN
(The Forsaken Maiden)

Eduard Friedrich Mörike
English translation by Joan Boytim

Hugo Wolf

Früh, wann die Häh - ne krähn,
Ear - ly the day a-wakes

eh' die Stern-lein schwin - den, muss ich am Her - de stehn, muss Feu - er zün - den.
and the stars are fad - ing, Now by the hearth I stand, kind - ling the warm fire.

Schön ist der Flam-men Schein, es sprin-gen die Fun - ken; ich schau-e
Bright is the fla-ming light, the sparks are fly-ing; I gaze con-

so da-rein, in Leid ver-sun - ken.
tin-ual-ly, en-gulfed in sor - row.

etwas lebhafter

etwas ruhiger

Plötz-lich, da kommt es mir, treu-lo-ser Kna-be, dass ich die
Ah, then, it comes to me, ah, faith-less lov-er, that I have

Nacht von dir ge-träu-met ha-be.
dreamed of you, the dream is o-ver.

wie zu Anfang

Trä-ne auf Trä-ne dann stür-zet her-nie-der; so kommt der Tag her-an
Tears af-ter tears now fall, blind-ing my tired eyes. So comes the day a-long,

o ging' er wie-der!
o, please be end-ed!

VIEILLE CHANSON

(Old Song)

Millevoye
English Version by Henry Chapman

Georges Bizet

don ___ que j'au-rai fait ___ Que de bai - sers, ___ que de bai
prize ___ as rare as this is, What lots of kiss - es, what lots of

sers! ___ Si ma Lu - cet - te, si ma Lu - cet - te
kiss - es! For if my dar-ling al - ways will pay ___

M'en don-ne deux pour un bou - quet, ___ J'en au - rai dix, ___ j'en au - rai
Two kiss-es just for a bou - quet, ___ I shall have ten, ___ I shall have

dix, ah! _____ J'en au - rai dix pour la fau-
ten, ah! _____ I shall have ten for you, my

vet - - te.
star - - ling!

La fau - vet - - te dans le val -
Now the star - - ling down in the

lon ___ A lais - sé son a - mi fi - dè - le, Et tant
dell ___ Had her - self left a faith - ful lov - er, And she

fait, tant fait, tant fait, que de sa pri -
strove so hard, tant so hard, that it soon be -

son El - le___ s'é - chappe à___ ti - re d'ai - - le.
fell, She did___ her lib - er - ty___ re - cov - - er.

Ah! dit le ber - ger dé - so - lé,_____ A - dieu les bai - sers de Lu -
Ah! cried the shepherd in dis - may,_____ Good - bye to kiss - es from my

cet - te! Tout mon bon - heur_____ s'est en - vo - lé___ Sur_ les
dar - ling! Now all my luck_____ has flown a - way___ On_ your

ai - les_____ de la fau - vet - te! Myr -
wings,_____ you wretch - ed star - ling! Once

til retourne au bois voi - sin,___ Pleu - rant la per - te qu'il a
more a-hunt-ing Myr-til went,___ Yet sad for what he failed to

fai - - - te. Soit par ha - sard, soit à des -
get___ her. Ei - ther by chance or by in -

sein, Dans le bois se trou-vait Lu - cet - - te,
tent, In the wood, there was his Lu - cet - - te;

Et sen-si-ble à ce ga - ge de foi,___
And so, when she saw how true was the lad,___

LA ZINGARA
(The Gypsy Maid)

Carlo Guaita
English Version by Theodore Baker

Gaetano Donizetti

La zin-ga-ra! la zin-ga-ra! Ah! _____
The Gyp-sy-maid! the Gyp-sy-maid!

Fra l'er - be co - spar - se di
Where chill dews of morn - ing on

ro - ri - do ge - lo, co - ver - ta dal so - lo gran
grass - es were gleam - ing, For cov - er and shel - ter the

TO THE BIRDS

(A des Oiseaux)

Eugène Adenis
English version by Louise Baum

Georges Hüe

How d'you do, my pret-ty thrush - es, Give you
Bon-jour, bon-jour les fau - vet - tes, Bon-jour

all a kind good-day! Haste to set the brook with
les joy-eux pin - sons, E - veil - les les pâ - que-

Printed in the U.S.A. by G. Schirmer, Inc.

rush - - es, Set the fields a - flush with May! _____
ret - - tes Et les fleurs des verts buis - sons! _____

While in hap-py cheer you hov - - er,   Pret-ty birds, so brave and
Tou-jours votre âme est en fê - - te,   Gais oi-seaux qu'on aime à

bright, _____   To the po - et and the lov - -
voir, _____   Pour l'a - mant et le po - è - -

er, Sing your song at dawn or night! _____   O - ver
te, Vous chan - tez ma - tin et soir! _____   Mais dans

yon-der in the heath-er, They have hid a cru-el snare; Swing in cir-cles there to-
la plaine, il me sem-ble Qu'on a ten-du des ré-seaux; Vol-ti-ger tou-jours en-

geth - - er, But, com-rades, Oh, have a care!
sem - - ble: En gar - de, pe-tits oi-seaux!

Dip and dive a-bove the stub - ble, But a-
Penchez-vous sans toucher ter - re, Voy-ez-

light not, for they wait! They will get you in-to trou-ble, Lure you to a sor-ry
vous au coin du bois, Vous guet-tant a-vec mys - tè - re, Ces en-fants à l'œil sour-

128